西蒙·拜爾斯

Heroes and Role Models | Non-Fiction Series

Copyright © 2022 by Level Learning, INC. and Washington Yu Ying PCS™
Original and Edited Text Copyright © 2022 by Washington Yu Ying PCS™

All rights reserved. No part of this book in whole or part may be reproduced without written permission from the publisher.

Published by Level Learning, INC.

Content Contributors:
Washington Yu Ying PCS™ - Aini Fang, Pearl Zao He You
Level Learning - Jingyao Qi

Illustrations by: Matt Austin

Leveling classification based on Level Learning standard.
For full description, visit www.levellearning.com

ISBN 978-1-64040-048-1
Traditional Chinese Edition

About Level Learning:
Level Learning provides a literacy focused curriculum specifically designed for K-12 Chinese as a Second Language classrooms. Our program offers 20 levels of specific and detailed objectives, leveled texts and passages, mastery-based online assessment, and analytics to enable data-driven instruction. Level Learning reading curriculum for both literature and informational text emphasize grammar and comprehension skills to help teachers develop confident and independent Chinese language readers. The non-fiction series of books are specifically designed to support our informational text course based on multiple national standards. To learn more about our entire offering, visit www.levellearning.com.

About Washington Yu Ying PCS™:
Washington Yu Ying PCS is a Mandarin English dual language immersion International Baccalaureate (IB) World school. Yu Ying's mission is to inspire and prepare young people to create a better world by challenging them to reach their full potential in a nurturing Chinese/English educational environment. Yu Ying's comprehensive IB, dual immersion curriculum equips students with global competencies for success in the real world. As a leader in immersion education, Yu Ying is determined to advance Chinese language programs and global citizenry education by helping other schools create and strengthen their Chinese programs. For more information, email: products@washingtonyuying.org

美國有一位體操運動員,她的名字叫西蒙·拜爾斯。

西蒙小時候和外公外婆住在一起。

西蒙愛她的家人。西蒙的家人也愛她。

西蒙六歲的時候開始練習體操。她把體操動作做得非常好。

西蒙十九歲的時候拿到了奧運會金牌。

西蒙非常喜歡體操。

西蒙還想再參加奧運會，想拿更多的金牌。

Glossary

	Pinyin	English Definition
體操	tǐ cāo	gymnastics
運動員	yùn dòng yuán	athlete
一起	yì qǐ	together
開始	kāi shǐ	start
練習	liàn xí	to practice
動作	dòng zuò	action, movement
得	de	structural word, particle
奧運會	ào yùn huì	Olympic Games
金牌	jīn pái	gold medal

www.ingramcontent.com/pod-product-compliance
Lightning Source LLC
Chambersburg PA
CBHW041226070526
44584CB00001B/118